Estelle & Ziggy

By: Adam DeRose

ISBN-13: 978-0692751176 (Custom Universal)
ISBN: 0692751173

"God was always with me."

—*Ziggy Janus*

To Estelle and Ziggy,

Thank you for everything you have taught me

and for being a major part of my life!

Thank you to Mom for helping me fill in the gaps to Estelle and Ziggy's life story.

Thank you to Aunt Kathy for finding the family photos for this story.

Thank you to Crystal MM Burton for her hard work and editing.

Without your help, I could never have finished this work of art!

Contents

Introduction

I met Stella and Ziggy Janus in April of 1984. I don't remember the details of the visit, but I know it went well, unaware of who they were and their ultimate impact on my life.

Ziggy always said he could write a book about his life's journey. At ninety years old, he has yet to put pen to paper, so I'm attempting to write his story for the benefit of future generations. Through a blend of recorded interviews, oral recollections, some of his writings and emails, I proudly present you the life of Zigmund Janus!

Chapter 1
Ziggy

"I could write a book about my life!"—Zigmund Janus.

I listened to his stories for years. Some details changed over time—much like the size of that fish caught by the proverbial fisherman—but those details never deterred much from the raw truth and history of the stories.

On a cold Saturday evening in October 2008, while visiting Ziggy at his home, I asked him to share with me the story of his life.

"I was born in Tczew, Poland," he told me. *"Right on the River Vistula. That's the main river that goes right through Poland, from Krakow up to the Baltic Sea. My birthday was July the 9th, 1925."* At the time, Tczew was a part of the Free City of Danzig, which had been created after World War I in the Treaty of Versailles. The area contained a blend of Poles and Germans, but it was not without hostility. Some ethnic Germans resented being forced to live among the Poles. According to Ziggy, *"The Poles controlled the services of the area, like the post office, transit, and the port. The German people still did technical jobs like engineering."*

Zigmund was born to Antoinette and Leo Janus. Leo worked on the trains as a conductor and Antoinette *"was a writer, a stenographer in the court. I think that's where I get my writing from."* On June 19, 1927, when Ziggy was two years old, his younger sister Zosia was born.

That same year, Antoinette, died of typhoid. She had drunk unpasteurized milk and fell ill with a high fever. Penicillin would not be discovered until 1942 when it was used to treat infections, so, sadly, Ziggy's mom passed away.

Shortly after Antoinette's passing, a neighbor introduced Ziggy's father to his sister. The sister lived up north in the town of Kartuzy. Eventually Leo and this lady became acquainted and ultimately married. They later had four children—Janek, Gainya, Helena (Helunia), and Yaninka.

Ziggy's paternal grandmother—who lived in Skarszewy with her second husband— told her son that she would raise Ziggy for him. Young Ziggy felt sorry for his grandfather, a plumber, because he was up in age and with no mode of transportation for work, he had to walk to his jobs. This was especially tough during the harsh Polish winters. Making matters worse, his grandfather did not walk well. He had been wounded in France while serving in the German Army in World War I. Ziggy vividly recalled that his grandfather's right leg was wounded, having pieces of shrapnel protruding through the skin. When he became old enough, Ziggy accompanied his grandfather to work, helping him out.

The small family lived in poverty, and even at a young age, Ziggy was well aware of his family's impoverished conditions.

Despite their living conditions, he still found ways to enjoy his life. One of his favorite things to do as a child was fishing. He still remembers fishing on the outskirts of town with his grandfather. Ziggy would carry his passion for fishing throughout his entire life.

Ziggy was raised in a Catholic family. One time, as the family got ready for church, he told his grandparents he did not feel like going. His grandmother did not want to hear that, so she dragged Ziggy right down to church and made him tell the priest what he told her. He said he felt so ashamed and embarrassed that he never mentioned his displeasure with church to her ever again. It turned out that a couple years later, Ziggy joined the choir and became an altar server, which he thoroughly enjoyed, especially around Christmas!

During Lent, the priest and altar servers would go around town and visit the parishioners at their homes. Each family would welcome them in with a nice warm feast. Ziggy was thankful and enjoyed the meals. He always cared about his grandparents, so he would bring home some extra pieces of food, such as cakes. The priest would bless each house and the residents would give him a monetary donation. During these Christmas visits, Ziggy got to meet a lot of people in his town, often times learning more about them than he anticipated. He laughingly recalled the women complaining to the priest about their husbands.

In his youth, Ziggy enjoyed going to school. Classes were five days a week and occasionally on Saturday. Growing up in Poland, Polish was Ziggy's first language. His grandmother, however, was bilingual. She would occasionally have friends over at the house and whenever she would want to tell something to her friend without Ziggy knowing what was being said, she would speak German. Ziggy said he would be there with his Polish/German translation book, trying to figure out what the old ladies were talking about. As a teenager, Ziggy spent a year and a half taking classes to learn to reads and write German. He always felt, *"If you want to move forward in life, you need to learn the language, otherwise you will be mistreated."*

At the age of fourteen, Ziggy remembered when the Germans moved into Poland in the Invasion of Poland, September 1939; the dawn of World War II. Shortly after the invasion, the Soviet Union and Nazi Germany divided Poland in half.

After Hitler and the Germans overtook Poland, Ziggy said the poverty was even worse at home. Since they did not have a television, he and his grandparents received news about the invasions and upcoming war via radio. He recalls that they received government-issued food stamps, which included a dozen eggs a week, but still was not enough food, and whatever food *was* available was rationed. He and his family were no strangers to real hunger.

"Well, Hitler went through Skarszewy, where we lived, in one day without a single shot. As you know, there were quite a few German families living in town. Their children were going with me to the same Polish schools, but their parents were all for Hitler and [to] free Skarszewy from the Polish dominations. [After] the first few

weeks, the domineering law in Skarszewy [changed] the town to Schoeneck, and they started robbing all the rich Polish people, and farmers, and tried to evacuate us out from Skarszewy."

Ziggy, his grandparents, and the rest of the Poles in Skarszewy lived in fear in their own town for close to a year before they were removed by the Nazis. During that time, the German sympathizers murdered the town's Polish priests. Ziggy remembers, *"They even murdered the three young Polish priests! One was a red-head, [who] I usually helped in celebration daily in the holy Mass. They buried them outside of town in a Jewish cemetery...the red-headed priest was nice...one of the young German butchers, drinking beer in a bar, was telling his friends [about the priest and how the red-head] begged for his life!"* Ziggy used to be an altar server for his favorite red-headed priest. The two of them used to go fishing together.

Ziggy remembers the removal from Skarszewy well. His grandparents' names were on a "list," so all three of them were sent to Sarnaki by train. *"They organized lots of people to gather us in a homemade camp. A long train took us all the way to the middle of Poland on the second river Poland has, called Bug, and let us off there in the small town called Sarnaki."*

Sarnaki was on the outskirts of Warsaw. Ziggy continued, *"There, they unloaded us in the hands of the Polish authority—the mayor of the village. We were stranded in the mercy of the Polish who lived there, so we were the northern refugees."*

"That village took us all under its warm arm. [The mayor] said 'Follow me' and took us to a small house in which a nice single woman lived with a teenaged daughter. [The mayor] stayed by the entrance. I went and talked to the lady. Well, it took some time to persuade her, but the daughter liked my smiling face. So we were adopted and lived there for quite some time."

After *"[probably] six months or longer,"* Ziggy and his grandparents were sent on a train to an internment camp in Teresin for displaced Polish who could speak German.

While being a refugee, Ziggy tried to make the best of it.

There were several times when he would walk down to the market and beg for food from the farmers. Whatever pieces of food he received, he would rush back home and share with his grandparents.

With a passion for fishing, young Ziggy soon found a great fishing spot outside of the Niepokalanow monastery. While standing on the banks of the water, he caught a fish. As he was taking it off the hook, he was greeted by a priest. Father Maximillian Kolbe told Ziggy he couldn't catch fish in that water because it was dedicated to the people he helped at the monastery. Father Kolbe helped all refugees during the war—Polish, German, Catholic, and Jewish. Ziggy tossed the fish back into the water and left.

The war upset Ziggy's grandmother, so she wrote letters to Berlin. She penned her displeasure that her family was displaced, and told them how they were refugees even though her two sons fought for the Germans.

A letter was received and action was taken. After six months, the Germans moved Ziggy and his grandparents back "home" to Skarszewy.

Shortly thereafter, Ziggy's Uncle Pavel—his father's only sibling—came to visit him.

Years ago, his uncle lived in Danzig and met a girl from Hamburg, Germany. The two got married and moved to Hamburg. Pavel was eventually drafted into the German Armed Forces. At the time of the visit, his uncle was stationed to work the anti-aircraft guns on the back of trains. He did patrols from Berlin to Paris and he had spent time in Italy too. The visit was memorable for Ziggy because Pavel had brought him a gift...a bicycle! Ziggy was thrilled. The bike gave him freedom and opened new roads for exploration. He was also able to find new fishing spots.

In 1942, Ziggy received a letter from Berlin stating that every male born in 1925 was going to be drafted into the German Navy.

"I felt real bad, you know. I had two options—either go to the [German] navy or go into the forest on the ground with the Poles [and fight the Germans]. I was seventeen at that time. I was afraid.

16

Some of those Poles got captured and killed by the Germans. I had some buddies of mine and said, 'Let's go and see, maybe we could go and survive the navy,' and most of us did. There were others that were sent to fight the Russians. If I resisted, who knows what might have happened? I don't know, maybe concentration camp?"

After three or four weeks, Ziggy was sent to Belgium for boot camp. He had a physical and was evaluated by a German doctor. He had an issue with his nasal passages, so the doctor determined that he was unfit to serve in a U-Boat, the term for a German submarine.

Boot camp only lasted a month or two. *"Them [drill] instructors were something else. They had no sympathy for us!"* While there, Ziggy's leg became swollen and infected. He saw another doctor and was admitted to the infirmary; however, the infirmary was in Denmark. He was transported to the hospital by train.

Ziggy enjoyed his time at the hospital because he was treated nicely. He said there were a whole bunch of *"old timers"* at the hospital.

The whole time he was enlisted, Ziggy did not want to fight; he wanted no part in the war. One day, he struck up a conversation with the guy in the hospital bed next to him. That soldier did not want to fight either. He told Ziggy he had similar pimples and sores on his body. When he scratched them, they would spread. Ziggy thought it was a good idea to scratch his pimples too. The trick worked for a bit, and the pimples and sores spread. The doctor would check him every Friday. After a few weeks though, the medicine overcame the illness.

Always thinking, Ziggy decided to make buddy-buddy with the hospital cook. As it turned out, the cook needed a helper in the kitchen. Ziggy was able to buy himself an additional two weeks at the hospital by assisting the cook. He recalled helping to make *"delicious smoked eels!"*

Eventually, Ziggy got issued papers to serve on a ship in Le Havre, France. He was to take the train from Denmark, through Germany and Belgium, before arriving for duty.

On his way to France, he decided to see his Uncle Pavel in Brussels. Ziggy was able to finagle his way onto a train to Belgium. *"I was at the train station and I had a ticket for Le Havre, but I wanted to see my uncle in Brussels. Them Gestapo were on the train platform, patrolling the band way. If you looked suspicious, [the] Gestapo would hold you up. I did not want any trouble from them, so I hid in the bathroom until I heard the conductor yell, 'All aboard.' Then I ran out from the bathroom and hopped on the train."*

Ziggy made it safely to Brussels and enjoyed a short visit with his uncle.

Days later, he made his way to Le Havre. He served on a ship that was commandeered by the Germans. I asked Ziggy about the ship he served on, but he did not remember the name or numbers painted on the boat. After doing some research, I was able to narrow it down to three ships on which Ziggy could have served.

In September 1939, the Free French Navy ordered Flower Class Corvette warships to be built. The Invasion of France by the Germans happened during May 1940. Four of these Corvettes were confiscated by the Germans a month later, in June.

-PA1's intended French name was to be *Arquebuse*, it was completed on April 15, 1944.
-PA2's intended French name was to be *Hallebarde*, it was completed on November 10, 1943.
-PA3's intended French name was to be *Sabre*, it was completed on November 10, 1943.
-PA4's intended French name was to be *Poignard*, it was never completed because it was sunk in August 1944.

Ziggy was on the ship for one and a half years, so it would lead me to believe he either served on *PA2 (Hallebarde)* or *PA3 (Sabre)*. I sent Ziggy this information, but he still could not recall the details of the ship. I would like to think he served on the *PA3 (Sabre)*.

He first learned English by serving on the commandeered ally ship because all the gauges and instruments were written in

English. The Germans had put labels on the gauges so the German sailors knew how to read the instrumentation.

Early on in his military service, Ziggy took up smoking. All the servicemen received rations, which contained a pack of cigarettes. He wasn't a fan of the cigarettes, but he still smoked them. His smoking days only lasted a handful of weeks though; one of his comrades, who received care packages from his family, traded him chocolates for the smokes. From that moment on, Ziggy used his government-issued cigarettes for trade.

Serving on the ship, Ziggy had multiple jobs around the clock. The ship patrolled the French shore of the English Channel. His main job was as an ammunition man—to supply the gunners with ammunition. During night patrol, Ziggy operated a spot light for anti-aircraft.

It didn't always go smoothly, however. Some seamen had trouble with Ziggy. They picked up on his Danzig accent.

"One German guy said, 'He come from the Poloki (the Polish land). He's undervalued.'

"I told them, 'You must be crazy! I'm a sailor, just like you!'

"Well, they bunched together like a bunch of hoodlums, you know? But I spoke some pretty good German. I overheard them [saying], 'We have to beat up them Danzigers.' They were planning on it at night so the captain or no one would see.

"That night, I lay in my bunk. The guy on top was going to beat me up, but he was good to me, one of my friends, but I knew better. Anyway, I got upstairs, and to the right were the toilets. So I says, 'I try to save myself.' I went to the toilet.

"They went to the bed to find me and the bed was empty. So they looked all over. They got to the toilet [and saw me] and start yelling for me, but they couldn't make too much noise, middle of the night, because they would wake the rest of them. They never got me out. I sat there until it got light.

"What happened the next night, there was another guy on the other side they wanted to get, but he had one of them bayonets and he was waiting for them...he wasn't sleeping, so when they come and attack him, he stabbed 'em right in the chest!

"Well, they take him to the hospital and [their plan] all come out, so they all got punished. So they didn't beat up nobody! But those son of a pup from Berlin, they're something else! [They're] losing [the] war, but they still [shout,] 'We're going to win! We're going to win! First England, then America!'"

Ziggy didn't exactly enjoy his job. His ship was on the small side and in the big fights, it didn't stand a chance. He recalled, *"I was the ammunition man of the highest mast. There was a gunner, they always a youngster, they always want to shoot, which I never wanted to shoot at nothing, but I was loading the regular ammunition. We were shooting at anything in the sky or at ship, British or America. We were defending ourselves. I was the guy who supplied the ammunition...I never got wounded! But the guy shooting, he got shrapnel. He got taken away, but I don't know what happened to him...it was the 6th of June 1944.*

"And then you could see all the American armada, you know, the big cruisers. They were shelling us, you know. I would say the closest those shells came to us was ten or fifteen feet away from our ship. When a shell falls, you know, in the water, it creates a huge fountain. I would say ten, fifteen feet; the water bump way up there.

"I says to the old timers, 'Where is this water coming up?'

"And they said, 'Don't you know? See those cruisers out there? They're shelling at us. They are American cruisers'

"...but that [General] Rommel, you know, was the commander of that Invasion of Normandy [for the Germans]. So what he did, he must expect it. Le Havre was the heavy part, up in the hills the Germans has two 8mm guns. They were bigger guns than the ship could carry. When we were in distress, those two guns open up, and the American cruiser had to go backwards. They couldn't reach us, and that's what give us safe haven back to the harbor. And I don't remember going back out on the water no more! Because the invasion was on and we were too small fighting the big ships so we were in the harbor.

"[A week] after the June 6, 1944 British and American invasion of Normandy, I was on patrol with my German rifle. That night, the ship was supposed to go out [on patrol]." Instead, the

ship stayed in the harbor. *"I was a night guard with another sailor, watching over the big ship Europa. It was a long ship but [I never boarded the] Europa. That Europa was given after the war to France. I don't know for what. The French were a coward people in my estimation, never done any fighting.*

"It must have been about 1am when I heard the loud noise of planes coming over the English Channel."

Being unsure and fearful for his life and his crew, Ziggy woke up another sailor. He informed the sailor that he heard aircraft coming toward the harbor. The sailor reassured Ziggy it was nothing; the planes were going further inland and they were safe.

Ziggy went back to his patrol post on the ship's deck. Then he heard a voice calling his name. He turned around to find who was calling him, but he didn't see anyone. He called for the person, but no one came forth. Moments later, he heard the voice again, telling him to get off the ship.

"As soon as the forward planes hit the town of Le Havre, they dropped the candles called 'lightshpure.' The whole harbor light up like daylight and then the bombs started falling.

"By that time, I was in a nearby German bunker, which was not too far from the ship. It was a terrible feeling as the bombs shattered the German ships and harbor. On the far side, you could see the fire and exploding ships and storage facilities. The whole harbor was ablaze that night, but I and a few brave men escaped the ship after hearing my shouts about the fires on board.

"Eight of the young sailors that were fully asleep on that small ship of seventy-two men and four guns drowned, along with my belongings—including a nice German camera I had.

"When the smoke cleared the next morning, I went to see it. Covered with water were parts of the mast and some steel pieces of the antiaircraft guns. That was the end of my sailing." Ziggy's ship was sunk during the night of June 15, 1944.

"I was transferred to a small German infirmary in the hills near Le Havre. I was frightened and thought I was injured by some of the thousands of bits of shrapnel from the falling bombs. Luckily, I was okay and enjoyed a few days of being taken care of by the sympathetic German nurses.

"As there was no ship to go back to, I was transferred to Paris and assigned a new post. There were twenty of us sailors guarding the waterway on the River Seine, which flows from Paris north to the sea. The German Army was supplying the northern front with ammunition and supplies by barges, which sailed [up-river]. We lived on a small island in a French villa. It was a huge house with a lot of rooms, a big garden, fish pond, and a little forest. It was a beautiful place.

"There was a beautiful garden next door owned by a French couple. It was gorgeous living. A young French woman came from the small village and did our cooking and laundry. The sun shone and spring was in the air. Despite the war, France was blooming the June and July that I spent there.

"We were given a small anti-aircraft gun in case of an attack. We managed the locks [system on the water] with French help. The river was smooth on both sides of the small island and I liked it. I fished many times and put the small fish in the pond by the house." Ziggy used to fish with the army-supplied grenades. The grenades would explode and shock the fish and eels, causing them to float to the surface. He mentioned that the eels were good eating.

But even fishing in such a beautiful place could be a dangerous venture. "God was always on my side. When the bombs [were] falling, I was always safe. Even the [allied] bombs, they didn't hit me or any wounds. I remember I was outside fishing one time…you know those young pilots, doesn't matter who they are, they are something else, you know. I was fishing on that river they call the Seine, it was on Sunday morning around 10 o'clock, and there was an old barn. After a while, I was meant to go next to the barn; the barn was located close to the river. Here comes a single plane, with two tails. It was a British plane, and they dropped a couple bombs right on top of the barn! I guess there was nothing there, it was farm land. If I was by it, I'd probably get killed. God was always with me.

"I visited the beaches of Normandy many times when I was a sailor. It was all barbed wire and mines and concrete fortifications built by the German Navy. The Americans succeeded in capturing *the area. This prompted the Germans to retreat. Our orders from Paris were to destroy the anti-aircraft gun and get ready for evacuation to Germany.*

"There were three of us Polish boys within that twenty man installation on the river. One of them became sick and was taken to the hospital in Paris. There were now me and Bolek. Bolek was a strong young blond and found a Polish woman living in the village; Aniela was her name. She became 'well acquainted' with Bolek. She was originally from Krakow, Poland and married to a Czech who was a prisoner of war in Germany. He fought with the French Army which surrendered to the Germans."

Aniela was informed about the war and told Bolek and Ziggy, "The war is getting closer and closer to Paris. The Germans losing. The Germans lost the battle in Caen and the Americans are pushing forward. Most likely, they will tell you to go back to Germany, but I am willing to hide you—to keep you in the cellar or wherever I can."

One late night, Ziggy was on patrol of the villa with a French rifle. It was around 2am when a man in a coat approached the front gates. Ziggy spoke to the man in German. *"What do you want?"*

But the guy did not answer. Instead, he went back into the bushes.

Ziggy went back to the villa and woke up one of the soldiers who spoke French. Ziggy said, *"Come give me a hand. There is a guy who looks like he wants to enter this gate."*

The two went back down to the gate. Though they did not see the stranger in the coat, the soldier spoke some words aloud in French. Ziggy and his comrade heard and saw nothing. The soldier thought the stranger might have been a part of the resistance.

The next day, Ziggy and the rest of the German battalion received an order from Paris to march back to Germany. "Pack your bags and try to get on any trucks from the front lines headed back to Germany. Try to ride with them."

The commander asked the twenty men if anyone spoke French. One guy did, so they went off to the nearby village to find vehicles to commandeer.

Chapter 2
The Escape

"On the day of the retreat order from Paris, our commanding officer went to the village looking for a car so he could drive towards Germany. He found a car but the owner had destroyed the battery, so they decided to walk, hoping to get a ride from the retreating German infantry.

"While the commander was searching for a car, I took a boat and rowed from the second villa we lived in to the island across the way. I told my German buddy I was going to get some apples for the road, which was grew on the island garden. I parked my boat and immediately went into the villa. I was looking for leftover food and apples. What I found, I hid in the cellar for later use.

"I looked around for a hiding place where I could be safe. Finally, I found an old abandoned water tower next to the neighbor's house, over-grown with brush and vines. The steps going up to the tower were broken and rotted away, so I had to climb with my own French nine-bullet rifle and not make any noise as the French neighbors sat outside having lunch. I did not trust the French, as I thought they were collaborators, they had been given a bunch of gasoline by our commanding officer which they hid in a sand pile.

Ziggy had great luck and managed to reach his hiding spot without detection. *"God was with me again. It was tough going on the third floor of the water tower. Luck was enough, no noise and no fall. I climbed to the third deck, which was overgrown by vines. I lay down and listen."*

He lay there for an hour, hidden in the vine covered water tower, when he heard one of his German friends coming toward the house and shouting for him. "Zigmund! Zigmund, where are you?"

He didn't answer, instead laying still and quiet inside the water tower. He clutched his French rifle tightly in anticipation of being spotted, but neither of the two soldiers saw him. They soon left a relieved Ziggy alone in the darkness.

Ziggy had his German navy watch to keep track of the time, and as evening approached the 7pm mark, a thunderstorm brought a light rain. He decided to climb down and make his way toward the only bridge leading into the village. He had no choice; he had to cross the bridge. He worried the infantry may have posted a guard, but the area surrounding the bridge was clear. Slipping through the narrow alleys in the village as quietly as possible, he ran up to Aniela's house and tosses a stone at her window to get her attention.

"She opened the window and I shouted, 'Zigmund.' She came down and opened the door for me, asking me, 'Where is Bolek?' I did not know. Aniela welcomed me and gave me some coffee and I lay down and went to sleep.

"The next few days, I was working in a civilian suit given by Aniela's husband. The German infantry was still in retreat in the village. I went to the villa and retrieved all of the food I had hidden, but the rest of the belongings had been taken by the French Resistance movement." Ziggy stayed with Aniela for about a week and a half.

"Finally, the Germans moved out of the village, so the French Resistance took over. Aniela informed them that she had a Polish young man who escaped from the German Navy. They came and took me and were polite, as I was a Pole. They fed me and kept me in one of their houses."

During the war, as Germany invaded different countries, they took over factories. The Germans forced the civilians to work in these camps to help their war effort. Ziggy was eventually moved to a Russian working camp outside of town.

"There I met Bolek again. The French Resistance captured him in that villa forest." Bolek had decided to defect from the German Service as well. He had hidden in an outhouse at the villa for three hours before finally being discovered by the French Resistance. *"The French found him and they said, 'There's another German pig!'*

Bolek raised his hands up and said, 'Polonaise, don't shoot!'"

The French Resistance got a Polish interpreter and Bolek explained to them that he was Polish and that he had a Polish buddy too, but he did not know what happened to him. He added that he met a Polish girl in town who might know where his friend Ziggy went.

After being at the Russian camp for about two weeks, a recruiter arrived, trying to persuade the young men to join the Russian forces. Ziggy told Bolek, *"They must be crazy! Fighting with the Russians! I'm not doing [it]."*

"As the war was deeper in Germany, the Polish Exile Army had a headquarters in Paris and was looking for volunteers to join the ranks of General MacArthur fighting the Germans in Holland and later on in Germany like taking the cities of Breda and Willenshafen."

Aniela was very concerned about her Polish friends. She contacted the Polish exile embassy and told them that there were two Poles in the Russian working camp.

A few days later, two Polish service men arrived at the camp and were looked for Ziggy and Bolek. Ziggy and the rest of the Russians told the Polish service men, *"No Poles here, only Russians!"*

Later, Ziggy told Bolek the Polish Army was looking for them. Bolek sounded excited until Ziggy told him he sent them away. Ziggy said, *"I don't want to go to no more army. I got enough fighting for somebody else."*

Bolek disagreed and said, "Oh no. We have to get out of here...I'll be watching the gate."

Bolek talked to Aniela, who convinced the Polish Army to return to the camp for Bolek and Ziggy.

The following day, Bolek spotted the Polish Army soldiers and he did all the talking while Ziggy stayed quiet. Ziggy was not interested in more fighting, but he conceded that he also didn't want to be fighting for the Russians on Russian soil.

"Aniela gave us a goodbye for me and my sailor friend, Bolek. We were taken by truck to Paris to join the Polish Volunteer Army stationed with its exile government in London, England. We stayed a few days in this big building called 'Koszary Bezer.' There were quite a few young men, both French and Polish. They all spoke Polish with a French accent. They were eager to fight the Germans and free Poland from the occupation.

"Bolek and I were on the first truck transport heading north from Paris to Le Havre. Everything was ruined; the roads were full of mines—right and left—you know, from the Germans.

"The journey from Paris to the ships took about four to five days, as we had to lay over for the night and the driver stopped a German prisoner of war. Well, he got food, and we were not treated too good by the Americans, as most of us were escapees or prisoners of war with the French civilians. I got along with the Germans in the camp as I spoke the language. The French and the rest of the Poles resented it, as they thought we would be shipped at better conditions.

"We finally got back to Le Havre, where we took one of those American landing crafts to England.

"And the English are a son of a gun too…they made us go to a boot camp. Once we got to England, the Polish officers who were with us surrendered us to the British for a shave and new British military clothing. They demanded that we surrender all the possessions we had and gave us a slip of paper to claim it later, but nobody did, and it was lost. The British even asked us for some of the French money we had with us; typical uncivilized behavior by the British staff. They also asked us about the German boat we were on and what happened to it."

Finally, they were returned to Polish hands. The Polish officers took care of Ziggy and the others and boarded them onto a train heading to Scotland. In Glasgow, Polish military trucks waited to take them to a Polish camp. There, they were given as much bread as they could want. Ziggy had been so hungry that he ate one and a half loaves by himself. They were given barracks and had their first peaceful night in a long time. The next morning, they were asked by the Polish officer identify themselves and most were given the same rank they had attained during their time in the German Navy.

"Me and Bolek asked to be inducted into the Polish Navy, which had four ships in England. Bolek was accepted by the doctor but I was rejected. They needed strong, built men.

"So I was assigned to an anti-aircraft platoon and sent for training in Scotland. Later on, I volunteered for driving a truck and I finally was assigned to a maintenance depot as a helper—truck mechanic."

After the European Theater ended, one of Ziggy's jobs was to gather unused artillery. Some of the unused weapons were taken to a secure location and detonated.

"I had a good life in the Polish Army. I volunteered for a few courses and spent sixteen weeks driving English trucks on the left side of the road. I attended thirteen weeks of a book keeping course and helped as a cook in one of the camps."

☺

Ziggy met his best friend, Gerry, in the Polish Army in Scotland. *"It is nice to have a person you can trust and rely on. That was Gerry to me, and I liked to help him.*

"Our chemistries jived and we became close friends while we both served under General Stanislaw Maczek, a Polish general."

Gerry was born in the port city of Gdansk. After World War I, Gdansk was created as a city-state. Its main occupants were Poles and Germans, and to that end, Gerry's mother was Polish and his father was German. He grew up in the small village of Gdynia.

Gerry and Ziggy were in Wales when they were finally discharged from the Polish Army.

After the war, they had the option to return to Poland, but both decided to stay in England. They felt that post-war life in England was better than in Poland. They both agreed there was nothing for them back there.

Additionally, there was no one for Ziggy back in Poland. During the war, Ziggy received a telegram that his father had died. His father was working as a conductor on the trains, and while en route to Warsaw, it was bombed. Also, Uncle Pavel and his grandparents did not survive the war. He had his sister, Zosia, and his half-siblings, but he was not close with them.

Lastly, they did not want to go back to Communism. Gerry and Ziggy had fallen in love with the freedoms of England. The two buddies made their way up to Middlesbrough, where they found work as mechanics. They were hired by a Japanese man, working on small British cars, BSA motorcycles, and the left-over US war trucks. After the war, instead of shipping all the American vehicles back across the pond, the US war trucks were auctioned off in England.

Ziggy had always looked out for his friend Gerry. Gerry was a smoker, and Ziggy told him not to smoke. Gerry reassured him that it was safe because the cigarettes he smoked had a filter on them.

Gerry had a knack for learning and adjusted well to the English way of life. It did not take him long to adopt the English accent. Whenever Gerry and Ziggy would go out for a night on the town, mainly to the ballrooms for dancing, he would tell Ziggy that he would do the talking and break the ice with the ladies first.

Ziggy enjoyed ballroom dancing; he liked it so much that he took classes so that he could impress the ladies at the local dance parlors. After dancing, Ziggy would take his lady friends out for fish and chips. Sometimes there was an occasional stroll through a cemetery, where they could be intimate, and not worry about being caught.

Even though Gerry and Ziggy were employed, they were both poor and shared an apartment. *"The land lady liked gambling on the jockeys. She was lucky; she asked me every morning to look up the famous jockeys in the morning paper and then she placed the bet. Between the winnings and our weekly rent, she made her living. And on the weekend, she went to the bar drinking with lots of her lady friends and boyfriend and had a wonderful time singing the old timers songs, such as 'It's a Long Way to Tipperary.'"*

Ziggy didn't have the luck of his landlady, and so he always worked two jobs. Besides being a mechanic, he worked as the conductor on the double-decker buses. His job was to collect the fare. There were many times where the bus company would conduct audits and check up on Ziggy, but he always had the correct amount. *"I liked the job. It was pretty exciting and it paid pretty good too. Union job. I would go up and down the stairs to collect fares. Always overtime around the holidays. Triple pay for me; two times for the holiday and one time because it was my day off. I worked Christmas and Easter. I always liked the Union and pension!"*

Chapter 3
Coming to America

Though Ziggy enjoyed his time in England, he wasn't 100% happy with it. At the time, there were about two million Catholics living there and he wanted to settle down with a nice Catholic girl (he also promised his grandma that he would settle down with a nice Polish girl). He figured the odds were against him. Young and single, Ziggy thought about exploring different lands because he *"didn't care too much for England."*

New Zealand popped into his head, but since Ziggy did not have any relatives there, he knew he wouldn't be granted a visa.

"I could have gone to Australia, but that's where England put all its prisoners, so I didn't want to go there."

Canada was welcoming the exiled Poles, but Ziggy didn't want to go there either.

He thought about Argentina because after the war, many Germans emigrated there. But, Ziggy found out that it wasn't too good there. Even though he was granted a visa to Argentina, he decided not to go.

One day in the fall of 1951, while working as the money collector on the double decker buses, Ziggy came across *Dziennik dla Wszystkich (Everybody's Daily)*, which was America's largest Polish newspaper based in Buffalo, New York. He grabbed that paper and took it home with him; he read that it cover to cover.

Ziggy showed the paper to his friend Gerry, though Gerry did not seem interested. Ziggy tried to tell him the newspaper was another ticket to a new life—a life in America! Unfortunately, Gerry didn't have any ambition of going to America. By then, Gerry had found a girl, Roslyn, who he liked and thought about settling down with (Gerry would later marry Roslyn and have one daughter).

Ziggy tried to reason with his friend by telling him, "There are so many beautiful women in America! You should come with me and explore a new place. If you don't like it, then you can always come back to bonnie England." But Gerry wouldn't budge; he was happy with where he was in life.

A short time later, Ziggy decided to write a letter to the editor of that Polish American newspaper. In the letter, he wrote that he was a former Polish soldier of World War II and that he was looking for sponsorship to the United States of America.

After about two weeks, Ziggy received almost twenty letters from America. It turned out that the editor had received his letter and decided to publish it in the paper.

Ziggy had people from Chicago, Detroit, and Buffalo write him to say they would be his sponsor. He even had a man in Burbank, California, who said he had lodging for him, a job lined up for him at Boeing, and that he could even marry the man's daughter! Ziggy thought to himself that it was a nice gesture, but he wanted to find his own wife.

In the hopes of reaching his dream to go to America, Ziggy applied for a visa. During that time, he corresponded with a couple potential sponsors.

"The sponsor did not have to pay a penny. [I needed a] written document that I could show the embassy in London to prove I had a sponsor. The air fare would be paid by the army, wherever I chose—either going back to communist Poland or any other country (to which) I chose to emigrate."

With sponsorship lined up in America, Ziggy decided to embark on a life-changing journey; a journey that would take him to a foreign land, where he knew no one.

Before leaving his apartment in Scotland, he sold his bicycle to his boss, Mr. Carling, at the automotive garage. After saying goodbye to his buddy Gerry, Ziggy traveled down to London where he spent two weeks waiting for his trip to America.

Ziggy had two options of travel to America—ship or plane. As he got ready for his trip across the pond, he decided to buy a new suit case, a large trunk. He lugged around all of his belongings, from his clothing to all of his mechanic's tools. After getting the trunk, he realized it would not fit on the plane because it was too large; hence, he took a boat.

The voyage began in London, England, with Ziggy boarding the RMS Scythia. The trip across the Atlantic Ocean took three days and four nights.

His first sight of North America was Halifax, Nova Scotia, Canada. Though he had arrived in Canada, he had no intention on staying. There was a movement by the Canadian government to attract Polish immigrants, and he had heard there were a lot of Poles in Hamilton, Ontario, but Ziggy had his heart set on the United States.

Ziggy was amazed at the amount of cars in Halifax. He asked someone, "Who do all these cars belong to?"

The Canadian said, "To the workers."

"What do you mean the workers?" Ziggy asked.

The Canadian replied, "This is how people get around here. Everyone has a car."

Ziggy said, "Well, I've seen cars before, but there weren't this many in England. And there certainly weren't this many in Germany or Poland."

From Nova Scotia, Ziggy had an eight-hour train ride down to Montreal, Quebec. He was quite tired when he arrived in Montreal. While at the train station, he overheard four German men talking, so he walked up to them. *I didn't want them to know that I was a Pole, so I spoke German to them so they would think that I was one of them. I told them that I was tired from traveling all day and needed some lodging for the night. They were nice to me and took me to the place they were staying at.*

"The caretaker wasn't too happy that another 'German' was staying with her, but she sure liked the money. As she walked down the hall to show me my room, she swore and cussed. She didn't know that I knew English and could understand her. Well, I found out later that she didn't like Germans because her brother got killed in the war by the Germans.

"I was only staying the night, but I think the caretaker thought I was spending a week. I felt sorry for that lady, so the next day when I left, I left her my watch on the night stand."

From Montreal, Ziggy had a one-way ticket for Detroit, which he didn't realize until he arrived at the train station. He had wanted to stop in Buffalo first and meet the one sponsor from Perry, New York—Mr. Jablonski. It was too much work for Ziggy to get his ticket exchanged for Buffalo. Instead, he sent a telegram to Mr. Jablonski, telling him that he was going to go to Detroit first.

When the train crossed over into the United States, it stopped for customs. A customs officer checked out Ziggy's paper-work and asked him if he anything to declare. Ziggy said that he was bringing a radio from England for his sponsor. *"That was the wrong thing to tell them. Those son of a guns held me and the whole train up for twenty minutes. Finally, they thought it was okay for me to have the radio."*

Eventually, Ziggy arrived in Detroit in January of 1952 and he was not a fan of the area. *"It was too busy. There were too many cars everywhere—and I thought Halifax had a lot of cars. Also, Detroit seemed like a dirty city to me. I met the potential sponsor there in Detroit. I liked the man, he was nice, but I did not like the wife. She seemed mean and cold to me. I was in Detroit for about a week, but I couldn't find a job."*

Not wanting to be tied down in one place, and having a huge country to explore, Ziggy decided to go to Perry, New York and meet Mr. Jablonski.

I wanted to go (to Chicago) too and see what it was like, but I never heard back from that sponsor there in the Windy City."

He first boarded a train, the New York Central, in Detroit en route to Buffalo. Along the way, Ziggy stopped off in Erie, Pennsylvania, to meet another potential sponsor.

Before arriving in Buffalo, Ziggy sent another telegram to Mr. Jablonski telling him he was coming.

His train arrived at Buffalo Central Terminal around 10am. Ziggy quickly learned that Mr. Jablonski never got his telegram, because he was not there to pick him up. He eventually made his way down to Perry, and yes, Mr. Jablonski was grateful for the radio that Ziggy had brought him.

Mr. Jablonski was the village milkman. For the first couple days, Ziggy would wake up at 5am and help his sponsor deliver the milk. It took about two hours to do the entire route.

The sponsor tried to help him find work in Perry, but because it was such a small town, work was hard to come by. Ziggy enjoyed Perry because not too far away was Silver Lake, a place that he often visited to go fishing.

Ziggy didn't miss the fact that Mr. Jablonski *"had not a bad-looking daughter. We corresponded with each other, but the romance fizzed out."*

In regards to work, Mr. Jablonski told Ziggy that he had an aunt, Mrs. Zygouli, who lived in Lackawanna, New York—a town just south of Buffalo—who Ziggy could stay with.

He also had another relative in Lackawanna who worked in the body shop at L.B. Smith, a Ford dealership on Abbott Road.

Mr. Jablonski's relative told Ziggy he would help him get a job as a mechanic at the dealership. However, there was a small problem; the relative liked his booze better than work. Payday was on a Wednesday, which meant the relative would drink away Wednesday afternoon and all day Thursday or until his paycheck ran out. He usually returned to work on Friday.

Ziggy met the relative on a Wednesday afternoon, but by then, the relative did not have work on the mind, only the bar. Ziggy figured the two of them would go on Thursday to see if he could get a job at the dealership; that never happened because the friend spent the whole day in the bar. Finally, on Friday, the relative took Ziggy to L. B. Smith to see if they would hire him as a mechanic. The shop foreman was a little hesitant to hire Ziggy because he was associated with the relative. After reassuring the foreman that he was nothing like the relative and that he desperately needed employment, Ziggy was hired on the spot.

While working at the dealership, Ziggy discovered a tool that he had never seen before—a ratchet. A few of the mechanics laughed at Ziggy and his tools that he brought over with him. Ziggy said, *"If I knew the American tools were so much better, then I would have sold my tools in England. I would have had less stuff to carry with me across the Atlantic."*

About a week later, Ziggy told his shop foreman that he needed a car. The foreman told him there were three 1949 Ford two-doors in the back lot; over the next three days, he took each car home and test drove them. Afterward, he told Ziggy which car he thought was the best of them.

"I was in the great and lovely country of ours for only three weeks before I had my very own car! It was a maroon 1949 Ford two-door!"

Ziggy stayed with Mr. Jablonski's aunt for about a year. Then he decided to move out and get himself an apartment.

He enjoyed his new place because it was close to Cazenovia Creek, where he could go fishing whenever he wanted.

One afternoon, one of Ziggy coworkers asked him if wanted to go to a tavern in South Park for some pizza. Ziggy asked, "What's pizza?"

The coworker said, "It's like a pancake, but they put pepperoni on it."

"Will there be beer?"

"Of course!" the coworker said.

"I really enjoyed that pizza. It was the first time I ever had it."

☺

"I had three dates in one day! The first girl lived in Black Rock, another on Gibson Street by the Broadway Market, and the third was in Lackawanna. I had to take them to different parts of town because I didn't want to accidently bump into (another) one. I liked them, but I didn't want to spend too much time with them and get too invested and tied down…"

☺

Just like in England, Ziggy held down two jobs in America. By day he was a mechanic, by night he was a broil cook at the Statler Tower in downtown Buffalo. He cooked everything from chops to seafood. *"Sometimes I would trade food for drinks with the waitresses."*

☺

Eventually Ziggy got bored of being a bachelor. *"I wanted to get married. First, I looked for girls in the tavern, but they were all drunk and dancing, and I said 'This isn't right for me. I have to find somebody my type.'"*

"I thought about going to California. I still had that potential sponsor out there in Burbank. I had a buddy that wanted to go to California too, but we couldn't agree on how to get out there. We both had cars, and he thought we should drive our cars out there. I didn't think that was wise. I told him that one of us should sell our car and we could ride together in one car; we could split the cost of gas. It was only seventeen cents a gallon. Well, we couldn't agree on anything.

"So, I knew a Polish priest from Poland at St. Peter and Paul. Father Alexi is his name now, but I told him (we spoke Polish), 'Father, I'm ready for California, this is my last try. I'm twenty-eight and I try to get married. I'm coming here on hardship. I'm having trouble trying to find them.'"

"Don't worry, Zigmund!" said the priest. "We got single dolly girls here!"

The priest found Ziggy a nice dark haired and skinned lady. *"I really like them dark-looking girls, the Spanish kind of girls or ones with dark eyes. I really liked her, but she didn't like me because she thought I was a Limey. The mother liked me, but I didn't want to marry the mother."*

Ziggy went back to Father Alexi. He told Ziggy the girl was not interested in him. Ziggy asked, "What is wrong with me? Am I too old for her?"

The priest said, "No, she wants an American boy."

"Oh," said Ziggy. "Good for her. I can't help it I wasn't born here."

The priest reassured Ziggy that he could help him out.

Juszkiewicz Family circa 1926
Left to right: Jane, Estelle, Maryanna, Andrzej, and Celia

Estelle's First Communion circa 1926

Skarszewy 1933 r.

Janus Family-1933

Grandmother   Sister Zosia   Step Grandfather   Father Leo   Ziggy

Estelle—circa 1940

Ziggy—circa 1941

1944c British Tank Army Unit

1945c British Tank Army Unit

1945c British Army Unit

Ziggy, British Army—1944

Ziggy with his New Imperial Motorcycle

1944-Ziggy and Gerry in Middleborough

Conductor Ziggy—circa 1948

Estelle and Ziggy-Wedding September 25, 1954

Estelle-Honeymoon NYC

Ziggy with his 1949 Ford

1964-Michael, Estelle, Ziggy, and Susan
Susan's 1st Communion

Circa 1987-Estelle, Kathryn, Adam, Ziggy, and Sarah

Ziggy, Estelle, Kathy, Michael—March 20, 1993

Left to Right: Hannah, Adam, Ziggy, Jonah, Nathan, and Alex—August 2014

Left to Right: Alex, Ziggy, Little Ziggy, Adam, and Alex
June 2016—1000 Islands

Ziggy and Annabelle—July 28, 2016

Chapter 4
Estelle

Estelle Regina was born on May 7, 1919 in Buffalo, New York, at her parents' house on South Division Street. Estelle had an older sister, Celia, and a younger sister, Jane.

Estelle's parents, Maryanna (Mary) Roman and Andrzej Juszkiewicz, emigrated separately from Poland to Buffalo. Though the two were both from Old Country, they did not meet until they were settled in Buffalo. They married in 1915.

For employment, Andrzej worked in a foundry—a dirty machine shop. However, that job did not last too long because it was during the Great Depression.

Meanwhile, Mary worked as a cleaner at the telephone company.

To help supplement their income, Andrzej and Maryanna bought a duplex on Seymour Street and rented out both units.

Estelle loved her father, though she was not a fan of his drinking. She felt as if her father were an alcoholic. He was strict with his daughters, but he was never mean or hit them. Every night, her father would make her and her sisters kneel and say their prayers to God before bed. The one thing that stuck out in her head was that her father once said, "I am not a father. I was given three girls. I don't have a son, so I do not feel like a father." Estelle said those words hurt.

During her childhood, despite her father's misgivings, her parents would take her and her sisters every Sunday after Mass to the park. They would take a street car from Seneca Street down to Cazenovia Park. They would pack a lunch, have a picnic, and spend the whole day there. Estelle said that many people didn't have cars back then, so people traveled by street car.

As kids, the Juszkiewicz girls grew up during the Great Depression. According to Estelle, she and her sisters knew that they were poor, but they did not care. The sisters made do with what they had and enjoyed their family. Estelle would talk about going down to the local nickelodeon and watching the Three Stooges.

The Juszkiewicz sisters attended Saints Peter and Paul School. After graduating from parochial school, Estelle attended high school for a couple years, though she wasn't interested in school. She went to Girls' Vocational for sewing.

Estelle's older sister Celia died at the age of eighteen. Celia was ill with TB and was sick for a long time in the hospital.

Estelle recounted that after her sister's passing, the family did not talk about Celia. However, Estelle remembered her sister being a very beautiful and smart girl.

Estelle was in her early twenties when the United States entered World War II. At the time, she was dating a nice young man named Peter. The two met while ballroom dancing at Peter and Paul on a Wednesday night. Peter's parents owned a tavern on Portman Street.

When Peter went off to the war, Estelle worked at a Curtiss airplane factory in Buffalo.

In 1952, Estelle's father passed away in the hospital during an appendix surgery.

Chapter 5
AND THEY MEET...

Estelle was active at Saints Peter and Paul Church and different societies. She was friends with the local priest.

One Sunday evening in January of 1953, the priest called Estelle on the phone at 9pm. He asked her if she could come down to the rectory.

Estelle was in her night gown, ready for bed. She asked him, "Why?"

The priest said he wanted to talk to her. Being the good Catholic girl that she was, Estelle decided to change clothes and walk down to the rectory.

Minutes later, she rang the doorbell. The priest answered and invited Estelle in, telling her to have a seat on the couch. Soon after, the doorbell rang again. The priest got up and opened the door.

According to Estelle, *"This guy walked in with these big eyes and I thought to myself, 'What's going on?!' And the priest invites this guy in and he comes and sits down right next to me on the couch! The guy talked to me and he was real friendly. When I left the rectory, I ran all the way back home!*

"The next day he called me...

"And the next day he called me...

"And the phone kept on ringing...

"He kept on bothering me, and that's how it all started."

☺

Ziggy knew Estelle would be at the rectory. In his version of the events, the meeting went much smoother.

"*Father Alexi said, 'Be here [at church] next Friday. I will have the girl here at 8 o'clock.'*

"*So I says, 'Okay Father, I'll be here.'*

"*So he calls Stella first. There was a long bench, you know, and I didn't know where to sit down, so I sat next to her. She thought I was fresh! And we started talking this and that, you know. The priest finally said 'that Ziggy wants to settle down.'*

"*Stella said, 'Well, you know, I have to work tomorrow and I have to get some sleep.' She ran from the rectory all the way home and I followed her.*

"*So the next day I called her, you know, to make a date.*" Their first date was to the Roosevelt Theater on Broadway—by the Broadway Market—to see a movie. "*After the movie, there was a restaurant, Deco. I guess it was Thursday or Wednesday, and I ran out of money and I didn't want to ask the landlady to borrow some. I asked Stella if she wanted to go for a cup of coffee, and she said, 'Yeah!' But she ordered some pastries and I ran out of money, so I asked her if I could borrow some money. She says, 'Oh yeah! I got some.' She always brings up that story...*"

☺

In Estelle's retelling of the date, after the show, Ziggy asked her, "Would you like to go to Deco for something to eat?"

She said that she would like a hamburger or a pastry.

Every time Estelle recounts the story, she **ALWAYS** *says*, "I should have known better!"

Ziggy said, "Oh, but you know what, I only have enough money for one hamburger."

To which Estelle blurted out, "Oh! That's all right! I've got money!" Estelle would always pause and jokingly follow the story up with, "Oh stupid me! That was a big mistake! And that's how it started."

☺

On the morning of September 25, 1954, Father Alexi married Estelle and Ziggy at St. Patrick's RC Church on South Division Street in Buffalo. It was a huge wedding. *"There were lots of people at the wedding that I didn't know,"* Ziggy said. *"Estelle had belonged to a few clubs and [had] lots of lady friends, so they were all there. I invited a few guys from the Ford dealership"* Unfortunately, Estelle's sister, Jane, was not a bridesmaid. At the time, it was tradition for single women to be bridesmaids. However, Jane's two daughters, Jackie and Joyce, were the flower girls.

Speaking about flowers, Ziggy had taken it upon himself to do the floral arrangements for the ceremony. Estelle wanted bouquets of roses done by a professional florist; she was not expecting Ziggy to order gladiolas from a local farmer. She was surprised by the flowers, but not in a good way.

Their wedding photos were taken in front of the Buffalo Historic Building, then the reception was held at the church. *"I enjoyed dancing to a very good Polish band. And the food was exceptional, made by the best cook lady from Saints Peter and Paul Parish. So it must have cost Busi—my mother in law—a mint. But it was fun to get married to a pretty girl I chose; a good Catholic Polish girl"* said Ziggy. He had held true to his word to his Grandmother about finding the right woman to settle down with. *"You know, everybody [wanted] the Polish food and all the drinks that went with it."*

After the wedding reception, the two took a flight to New York City and spent their honeymoon there; it was the first time they were on an airplane. For Estelle, it was also her first trip to NYC or even being on a subway. She was excited. The newlyweds enjoyed their getaway and did some sight-seeing and shopping.

☺

Since Estelle didn't know how to drive, Ziggy taught his new bride how to operate a manual transmission, practicing in his 1949 Ford.

"Every time I would do something wrong, Ziggy would bump my leg," Estelle recalled.

But learning to drive a stick isn't always easy on the vehicle. *"Estelle ended up breaking that transmission,"* Ziggy noted. *"Down in Lackawanna was a junk yard. I talked to the owner and asked him if he had any transmissions for a '49 Ford. He told me he had a few in the back and that I could look at them. I inspected them and tried to find the best one. I asked the owner, 'How much is it?' and he said, 'Ten dollars plus your old transmission.' I put that transmission in and the car rode nice."*

The experience at the junkyard went so well, Ziggy returned after his first accident when a car hit his door on Ridge Road. He didn't know how to fix it himself, so he went back to the junkyard and this time asked the owner if he had any doors for a maroon Ford. Luckily, as before, the owner said, "Yeah! There's a few in back." So Ziggy took a look and found a nice door. He asked the man how much he owed him and the owner said, "Ten dollars and your old door." It was a nice and easy fix and Ziggy didn't have to do any body work or painting.

☺

1957 turned out to be a good year for Estelle and Ziggy.

They were a part of the post-war urban sprawl. The two moved out of the city of Buffalo and into a newly built house on 35 Veterans Place in Cheektowaga in July 1957. It was a nice yellow brick ranch with a white three tab shingled roof. They chose that location because Estelle's sister, Jane, and her husband, Lenard, already lived on Veterans Place and liked the area. Ziggy enjoyed the corner lot, so he and Estelle purchased it. Since he was a mechanic by trade, Ziggy wanted a garage. He talked to the builder and was able to hatch a deal—$1,500 for a two-car garage and built-in patio.

Then, on July 8, 1957, Ziggy received his naturalization papers!

He went to the courthouse in downtown Buffalo and took a test. There were many questions, and quite a few were about American history.

Chapter 6
Family and Adventures

"I always worked two jobs," and that was something Ziggy was proud about. Throughout his career, Ziggy worked at L.B. Smith Ford, Dixie Ohio, Eastern Forwarding, Yurgi Motors, Tripi Foods, and his favorite job, working as a welder at the Niagara Frontier Transit Authority.

Ziggy first started working at the NFTA in 1957. *"I loved that job at the NFTA! It was better than working at the dealership. At the dealership, there was always a line of cars to work on, and the foreman was always hounding us to get the cars out the door. As soon as you would finish one car, there was another one to work on. I liked the bus garage and the union. If you didn't finish your job at the end of your shift, no worries. There was a huge fleet of buses, so they had extra ones."*

Ziggy enjoyed the job because there was opportunity for overtime. One Saturday morning, he was putting in some extra time at the garage. The phone in the shop rang a few times and Ziggy decided to run over to it and answer it. On his way over to the phone, he tried to jump over one of the pits, but he did not make it. He fell and broke a few ribs. He laid in the bottom of the pit before one of his coworkers found him. He recovered and happily went right back to work as soon as he was able.

Ziggy would later retire from the NFTA in 1990 with fond memories and great relationships.

☺

On August 2, 1957, Estelle and Ziggy welcomed their first child, a daughter named Susan. Two years later, on May 6, 1959, Estelle and Ziggy welcomed their second child, a son name Michael.

A couple years later, Estelle's mother Maryanna moved in

with Ziggy and Estelle to help take care of Susan and Michael. At the time, Estelle worked for Sylvania making light bulbs, so it was helpful to have someone stay home with the kids.

☺

It was during the mid-late 1960s when Ziggy discovered his second favorite place on earth, fishing in the 1000 Islands!

"Stella's sister Jane married that Lenard. Well he had two brothers. The one brother worked for the rail road company and he's the guy who introduced me to the 1000 Islands. He said, 'Let's go to 1000 Islands. It's quite a ways, but you'll love it!'"

Well, the rest is what they call history...Ziggy fell in love with the region and made multiple fishing trips a year up there.

Traveling became a steady part of life for the small family of four. Estelle and Ziggy took their kids Susan and Michael up to Montreal for the 1967 International and Universal Exposition, also known as Expo 67.

During the mid-70s, Ziggy took his family to Poland so they could meet the rest of their family, including Ziggy's sister Zosia.

During the mid-70s, Ziggy suffered his first heart attack. He had open heart surgery performed at Buffalo General Hospital.

The cardiologist told Ziggy that he needed to eat healthier. All the cold cuts that he was getting from the Broadway Market were clogging his arteries.

Ziggy tried listening to his cardiologist and made an attempt to eat healthier, but it was difficult.

☺

Besides the 1949 Ford 2 door, Ziggy's other favorite car was his AMC Rambler. He would rant and rave on how simple it was to work on and how he loved it. Besides the Rambler, he also owned a few Fords and Chevys.

Ziggy's son Michael liked the Rambler because he never had to work on it. However, Michael disliked the Chevys. "I hated working on that piece of junk! Oh my God, every weekend we were always fixing something on it! Because dad worked at a garage, he had access to a lift. He would always drag me with him so that I could help him and learn about cars. I learned about cars alright, that they are a pain in the [butt] to work on. Especially up here in Buffalo with all the salt during the winters. Everything rots on the cars and bolts rot or strip off. Yes, those Chevys were a huge pile and a headache. There were always something breaking. The exhaust pipe had more patches on it than actual stock pipe, but that was dad. He grew up in poverty, and as long as the thing worked, it was fine. Stuff didn't need to be pretty, as long as it functioned properly."

☺

On September 15, 1979, Estelle and Ziggy's daughter married Donald DeRose at St. Josepaht's Church on William Street in Cheektowaga.

Before the wedding, Donald and Susan had been dating for a while. As the story goes, Ziggy was watching a Buffalo Sabres hockey game when Donald asked Ziggy for Susan's hand in marriage. Ziggy, who was more focused on the game, said, *"Yeah, there's an axe in the garage."*

After getting married, Susan and Donald moved into an apartment on Grand Island, New York, which was about a half hour away from Estelle and Ziggy.

Susan and Donald welcomed their first child, Sarah, on February 3, 1981. Estelle and Ziggy were ecstatic to become grandparents for the first time.

Most importantly, I—Adam DeRose—was born on April 17, 1984. I'd like to think that Nana and Grandpa Ziggy were most excited about me being born out of all the grandkids!

A few years later, my parents blessed Nana and Grandpa Ziggy with another granddaughter, Kathryn was born on August 28, 1987.

Nana and Grandpa Ziggy loved being grandparents. They enjoyed every moment of watching us grow up.

Chapter 7
Traditions and Memories

I have very fond memories of Nana and Grandpa Ziggy. I remember spending countless hours during the spring, summer, fall, and winter at their house.

When I was a kid, my mom would drop me off at Nana and Grandpa Ziggy's house for the weekend. I would normally arrive on Friday night. If there wasn't a Buffalo Sabres game to watch on TV, then we were watching TGIF (Thank God It's Friday) on ABC. We would watch shows like *Family Matters, Perfect Strangers, Dinosaurs, Step by Step, Hangin' with Mr. Cooper, Boy Meets World,* and *Sabrina, the Teenage Witch.* We would cap the night off with *20/20,* but I usually fell asleep minutes into the show.

Saturday morning consisted of Grandpa Ziggy and me gallivanting all over Buffalo in his 1989 Chevrolet Caprice, ex-cop car. As we drove through the streets, Grandpa would stop and show me where he used to work, or where he almost had employment. He would also point out different buildings and tell me what businesses used to occupy the space. It was a pleasure listening to Grandpa talk about the old days.

Our first stop of the morning would be to the Super Flea and Farmer's Market on Walden Drive in Cheektowaga. The flea market was a wonderfully weird dump! That's where I got all my Buffalo Bills and Sabres cards and sports memorabilia. Grandpa Ziggy would always sell old hub caps that he found. Grandpa was always thinking and trying to make a buck. While the vendors were trying to peddle their stuff, Grandpa Ziggy would bring them old hatchets, tools, and hub caps and sell them to the vendors. He always made off like a bandit.

Next, we would go to the Broadway Market. Grandpa would pick up some rye bread, cold cuts, and horseradish. Later in the day,

Nana would always yell at Grandpa for picking up the cold cuts, due to his heart attacks.

Afterwards, we would sometimes get our hair cut. Grandpa had his favorite place. There was an old Italian guy—who looked like OJ's lawyer Robert Shapiro—on Grant Street, by Buffalo State College. I remember the scissors the old Italian guy used. I'm not sure if they were dull, or what the problem was, but those scissors didn't cut my hair. Those things plucked my hairs! I also remember that it didn't matter what kind of hair cut style I wanted. I was getting the hair cut style that he felt like giving me. It was always short and with a part. I liked that he did the hot shave with a real razor blade, though. He would always shave me high around the ears. Grandpa Ziggy like the place because the price was right—$2.50 a haircut, and that was during the mid-1990s. Grandpa Ziggy got a little upset when the old Italian guy raised his rates by $1. But I tell you what, that place was always packed on a Saturday!

After getting our haircuts, we would cap the morning off with a stop at the Clinton-Bailey Market. By the time we would arrive at the Clinton-Bailey Market, it would be around noon, and most of the vendors would be closing up shop. Grandpa Ziggy would always get good deals and bargains on plums, green beans, and other produce. Grandpa would make out like a bandit at this market too because he would sell the wooden produce baskets back to the farmers for a small price.

Whenever we passed by a tractor trailer, Grandpa Ziggy would tell me that he used to work on the big trucks. While working for the trucking outfits, he said that one of his jobs was to change the blown tires. He reminisced that the trucks would be stranded on the side of the highway with snow waist deep, and the blown tire would always be the inside tire. When he wasn't changing tires, he was doing routine maintenance on the trucks. He told me several times that he liked working on the trucks more than cars because they were easier to work on. *"The trucks are bigger than cars. They have bigger parts and are easier to get to than parts on cars."*

If it was summer time, on the ride home from the Clinton-Bailey Market, we would stop at every garage sale that we saw. Grandpa would have his eyes open for old junk he could make new and sell to the vendors at the markets.

By the time we got to the house, we would find Nana working on supper or pies for Bingo. I always thought it was weird that Nana and Grandpa Ziggy would call dinner *"supper."*

While she cooked, I would play with whatever video game I bought for my Sega Genesis, look through my sports cards, cut the grass, or climb the apple tree. Nana and Grandpa Ziggy had a couple pear trees, but they were off limits for me to climb because they were not sturdy enough for climbing.

Nana would always make a traditional Polish dinner with potatoes, cabbage, pierogies, green beans, and meat of some sort. I remember the house always smelling so good.

Supper would be around 3pm because we went 4pm Mass on St. Josaphat's on William Street. Grandpa Ziggy was an usher at church, so we always arrived at church fifteen minutes early. As a kid, I never really liked going to church, especially early. For the longest time, I thought that only old people lived in Cheektowaga. Every time I went to 4pm Mass with Nana and Grandpa Ziggy, the church was always filled with old people. I was the youngest person there by seventy years!

During Mass, I had no idea what was going on because it was all in Polish. I knew when the alter server rang the bells that it was almost time for communion.

One of the redeeming things about going to church was seeing Nana's sister Aunt Jane and her husband Uncle Joe!

It was a second marriage for Aunt Jane and Uncle Joe. Both of their spouses had died years ago. Grandpa Ziggy worked with Uncle Joe at the NFTA bus garage for years. Grandpa played match maker and got Jane and Joe together. Aunt Jane and Uncle Joe married when I was about three years old and they lived only five houses away from Nana and Grandpa Ziggy. I remember many times telling Nana that I was going to ride my big wheel down to Aunt Jane and Uncle Joe's house to visit them. They had a little yippee dog that my cousin Scott named Pee-Wee, after Pee-Wee Herman (this was well before Pee-Wee's "movie theater" incident).

Nana was very close with her sister Aunt Jane, or Janie as Nana called her. Nana and Grandpa Ziggy would go on many gambling trips with Aunt Jane and Uncle Joe. Most of the trips were put on by the Seniors group at Josaphat's.

Anyway, after church, we would go back to Nana and Grandpa's house.

If it was during the winter, Grandpa and I would watch the Buffalo Sabres game.

If was during the summer, Nana would take me to lawn fetes or to bingo. Lawn fetes were fund raisers that local parishes would have during the summer. There would be a beer tent with a live band, a Monte Carlo tent, pull tabs, other sorts of gambling, and chicken dinners. Some lawn fetes even had carnival rides.

Speaking about bingo, I remember playing bingo with Nana and Aunt Jane at the gymnasium at St. Josaphat's. Back then, one could some almost anywhere in New York State; and the church gym was no exception. I remember seeing a huge cloud of cigarette smoke hovering above the gym.

☺

For my entire life, Grandpa always drove Chevys. He always had an old highway patrol Chevrolet Caprice from North Carolina State Surplus. One of the things I remember about that Chevy was how the seat belt buckles burned during the summer. Grandpa's 1989 Caprice had the metal buckles and release latches. It seemed like it did not matter what time of year it was—just as long as the sun was beating down on the Chevy—those buckles were like touching a cherry red electric stove burner!

Grandpa Ziggy told me that he liked Ford motors, but he liked the size and shapes of Chevy better.

The Caprice was always the car we took up to 1000 Islands. Uncle Michael and Grandpa Ziggy would pack that car to the brim. Grandpa built the trailer hitch of the car while he was working at the NFTA bus garage. He would always borrow a boat from one of his buddies and we would pack the boat full of gear. We had at least two dozen bungee cords strapped across the boat, hold our gear down.

Every third week in June, Nana, Grandpa Ziggy, and Uncle Michael would make their yearly fishing trip up to 1000 Islands. I was about 7 or 8 years old the first time I went up.

Grandpa Ziggy liked fishing on the Canadian waters better than the American waters, not that I think the fish knew about the border. Anyway, before we would travel up to the Islands, Uncle Michael and Grandpa needed to get their Canadian Fishing Licenses. I would go across the border with them into Canada. This was well before 9/11 and the borders were very lax to the point where we did not need our birth certificates to cross. Anyway, we would always go to Canadian Tire to get the licenses.

On the way back, we would stop at Duty Free. Uncle Michael would pick up a few cases of Molson Brador, Molson XXX, and Molson Stock Ale. Grandpa would always pick up a carton or two of Marlboro cigarettes for his old buddy Gerry back in Bonnie Scotland. Grandpa would always tell me not to smoke because it would kill me. He told me that he would tell Gerry to quit smoking too, but Gerry would always tell him, "Don't worry Ziggy, the cigarettes have these filters on them, so they are OK." Needless to say, Gerry passed away from lung cancer.

Uncle Michael would always book a cabin on Wesley Island State Park. The one year we stayed at Dewolf Point State Park. Dewolf Point was more of a wilderness park, strictly fishing. Thankfully we only stayed there once.

I enjoyed Wesley Island State Park way more than Dewolf because there was more stuff going on. Wesley had a beach with a swimming area, a large red barn with an arcade, trails, and a canteen.

From the 14 foot aluminum boat, I could always see the 1000 Islands Skydeck. The Skydeck was a tower on the Canadian side that overlooked the region; a tourist trap for a lack of a better term. For years I always wanted to go up in the tower. Every year,

Grandpa Ziggy would tell me the same thing, *"We are up here to fish! Not to go to the tower. We are not here to sight see."* Needless to say, I have not visited the Skydeck yet.

☺

Every Christmas Eve was celebrated at Nana and Grandpa Ziggy's house. The party would start a little after 5pm because Nana, Grandpa, and Uncle Michael would always go to 4pm Christmas Eve Mass.

Grandpa Ziggy was an usher at the Saturday 4pm Masses and Christmas Eve 4pm Mass.

I remember the one year I got dropped off at Nana and Grandpa's house early, on December 23rd. On the 24th Grandpa took me to Mass with him at St. Josaphat's. I remember thinking that if I went to Christmas Eve Mass, then I would not have to wake up early on Christmas Day and go to that Mass. Well I thought wrong! I ended up going to both Masses, and I'm not going to lie, it sucked! No kid likes going to church, let alone twice in one weekend! I felt like Grandpa Ziggy when he was a kid and didn't feel like going to church. I presented my case to mom, but she didn't care; she still forced me to go to church. Thankfully she didn't make me tell the priest on Christmas morning that I didn't feel like going to Mass.

Anyway, back to the Christmas Eve celebration tradition. Nana's sister Aunt Jane and her family would come over. We would have a traditional Polish dinner. Uncle Michael would cook up the fish that we caught in 1000 Islands. Nana would make sauerkraut and potato pierogies from scratch. The family would partake in the Oplatki tradition. Oplatki wafers were purchased at church during Advent. At dinner, each person would have a wafer, and you would break off three pieces of someone's wafer while wishing them good luck or prosperity for the following new year. I would always wish for everyone to win the lottery.

Sometime during the evening—after dinner—Santa would show up! Nana and Grandpa didn't have a fireplace with a chimney, so Santa would have to come in through the side door. He would have presents for all the little boys and girls. After he got done delivering the presents, he would leave because he was on a very tight schedule!

☺

As a youngster, I told Nana that Steam's song "Na Na Hey Hey Kiss Him Goodbye" reminds me of her because the band says "Nana" several times throughout the song. She smiled. Whenever the song comes on the radio, I still think about her.

☺

Mom would drive my sisters and me to visit Nana and Grandpa Ziggy at least once a week. Whenever we would visit during the summer, Grandpa would almost always be working on one of the cars. He would dress in his one-piece denim mechanic suit. His Siamese cat, Nicholas, would be at his side. I thought Grandpa and Nicholas looked like Gargamel and Azrael from Hannah Barbara's animated cartoon, *The Smurfs*.

☺

Nana and Grandpa Ziggy had two pear trees and an apple tree growing in their side yard. Grandpa told me he had purchased those trees years ago at the Broadway Market. I enjoyed the apple tree because it was an excellent climbing tree for a kid, and because Grandpa made us a swing for the tree. I wasn't supposed to climb the pear trees since they weren't as sturdy as the apple tree. However, that didn't stop me from trying anyway. There were several times when Nana would yell at me from the kitchen window.

During the late summer and early fall, it was my job to pick up the apples and pears. Nana would make homemade apple and pear sauce, along with pies.

☺

During 1992, Grandpa Ziggy suffered his second heart attack. Personally, I think it was the Buffalo Bills Super Bowl XXVI loss that caused the heart attack.

Grandpa had another bypass surgery, but it was performed at Cleveland Clinic in Cleveland, OH. The surgery was a success, so our story continues!

To this day, if Grandpa Ziggy finds out someone needs heart work done, he instantly recommends the Cleveland Clinic.

☺

Grandpa Ziggy was always a huge Buffalo Sabres fan. There were many evenings when I wanted to watch cartoons, but instead, I ended up watching hockey with Grandpa.

It was the early 1990s when Grandpa Ziggy brought me to my first Buffalo Sabres game at the Memorial "the Aud" Auditorium. I don't remember how old I was, let alone who we played, but two things stuck out to me during that game.

First, I felt like I was going to fall down the stairs. The Aud's seating was very steep and I thought that if I wasn't sitting in my seat, then I would fall down the stairs, over the ledge, and onto the ice.

Second, Grandpa brought radishes as snacks. He may have liked them, but I thought they burned my tongue a little. I wanted something sweet and yummy, like candy; I ended up with vegetables.

Because of Grandpa Ziggy and his influence, I am a Buffalo Sabres fan.

As a kid, my only source of income was cutting lawns, shoveling driveways, and collecting bottles and cans. It would take me months to save up enough money to buy two hockey tickets in the 300 Level. When the Sabres moved from the Aud to Marine Midland Arena in 1997, the cheapest seat in the house was $13 (compared to $49 in the 2016-17 season).

I would save up enough money during middle school for one or two games a season.

During the mid-late '90s, Pizza Hut and the Sabres had a promotion where $80 would get you four tickets, two pizzas, and two souvenir pucks. The promotion only lasted a few seasons, but I would try to get tickets each year for a game around Christmas. It would be my Christmas present for Grandpa and Uncle Michael.

There are a few hockey games that I remember going to with Grandpa, but there is one that sticks out beyond the rest. For my birthday, I got a pair of tickets to the Ottawa Senators @ Buffalo Sabres, Round 1, Game 7 Playoff game. It was April 27, 1997 and Grandpa Ziggy and I were sitting in the 300 Level, right behind the net. Since it was Game 7, everything was on the line. The game was tied 2-2 and heading into overtime.

Just minutes into overtime, Buffalo's Derek Plante stole the puck, skated into the Ottawa zone, and blasted a slap shot past Senators goalie Ron Tugnutt to win the game 3-2! The play had unfolded right in front of us. The whole arena went wild. It was great!

☺

On March 20, 1993, Uncle Michael married my neighbor's daughter Kathy. The wedding was at St. Stephen's Church on Grand Island. Uncle Michael asked his father to be his best man. I was asked to be the ring bearer. I was eight years old and I did not enjoy wearing the monkey suit of a tux.

On June 9, 1997, Uncle Michael and Aunt Kathy welcomed their first son, Alexander, into the world. Nana and Grandpa Ziggy were thrilled to have another grandchild! Grandpa couldn't wait to take Alex up to 1000 Islands and teach him how to fish.

Uncle Michael and Aunt Kathy had a second child, Nathan, who was born on March 11, 1999. Nana and Grandpa Ziggy welcomed their fifth grandchild into the world with open arms.

Instantly, Grandpa started working on a college fund for Nathan, just like he did for the first four grandkids.

Grandpa loved watching and playing the stock market. Every day he was watching the ticker tape on TV. It felt like Grandpa was on the phone at least once a week with his stock broker (this was well before the explosion of the internet and online trading).

☺

We would celebrate birthdays as a family. When I was a kid, it felt like we were celebrating someone's birthday each month. Nana and Grandpa Ziggy had five grandchildren, while Aunt Jane had five grandchildren too.

It didn't matter whose birthday it was, but we always sang Sto lat.

> *Sto lat, sto lat,*
> *Neich zyje, zyje nam.*
> *Sto lat, sto lat, Neich zyje, zyje nam.*
> *Jeszcze raz, jeszcze raz,*
> *Niech zyje, zyje nam,*
> *Niech zyje nam!*

The song translates to "100 years, 100 years, may he/she live, live for us." Nana would always throw in an *"Olay!"* at the end.

☺

As a kid, Grandpa Ziggy often told me, *"My grandmother always told me, 'Ziggy, God gave you a brain! Use it, otherwise it will turn to weeds.'"* I try to remember that quote and use it throughout the day, especially when I was younger.

☺

One time I was visiting Nana and Grandpa Ziggy. We were on the couch in the sitting room. For some reason, Nana and

Grandpa got into an argument and they were bickering back and forth.

The conversation first started off in English and then quickly switched to Polish.

I thought they switched to Polish because they didn't want me to hear them swearing.

After they ended their argument Nana, "Why did you have to talk to Grandpa in Polish?"

"So he could hear better," Nana said.

☺

Nana loved going to ceramics. She would meet up with her friends and they would make ceramic figurines and holiday decorations. I remember for one of my birthdays, Nana made me Ninja Turtles figures. For another birthday, she made me a Buffalo Bills helmet bank! Throughout the years, she made each one of her grandchildren several different ceramic pieces from banks to music boxes.

Back in the late '90s, Nana was leaving her friend's house where she did ceramics. Nana ended up losing her balance and fell. She ended up spraining her wrist, but did not break anything.

Nana was 80 and she told mom that she was nervous because she was closing in on the same age as her mother Busi when she died. Mom tried to console Nana and told her that she had nothing to worry about. This was around the time when Nana told mom she wanted to stop driving.

☺

The Church and their faith in God and Jesus was a big part of their life. A lot of their social activities were through the church. Nana belonged to the Holy Name Society and Rosary Society. Grandpa belonged to the Knights of Columbus and he was an usher at Saturday 4pm Mass.

In 2006, Grandpa Ziggy won the Holy Name Society's Man of the Year Award. Mom joked around with Grandpa and told him that the Holy Name must have ran out of men to give the award to, which is why he won!

Additionally, they two were a part of Seniors. Through Seniors, they would take many gambling trips; most of them were to Atlantic City.

Grandpa Ziggy wasn't a big gambler; he preferred to play the stock market...though he enjoyed getting the free beer from the cocktail waitresses.

Nana, on the other hand, loved to play the one armed bandits. Grandpa would always scope out the other slot machines while Nana played. If he saw someone at a slot machine for a while, win nothing, get up, and leave, he would rush over to Nana and tell her to switch machines because he thought it was lucky.

☹

Speaking about gambling, Nana and Grandpa Ziggy had a trip set up in October 2003. They were to fly out at the end of the week to Las Vegas. They were to meet up with Uncle Michael and spend the week gambling and taking in the shows.

That Columbus Day, Nana called mom and told her she wasn't feeling well. Mom ended up taking Nana to South Buffalo Mercy Hospital. It turned out that Nana had a heart attack and needed open heart surgery.

The surgery, which was performed at Mercy Hospital, was a success. For rehab, Nana was transferred to Erie County Medical Center.

Nana was doing well with rehab and was on course to make a full recovery. A month or two later, Nana suffered a stroke. Thankfully she was able to recover from that too.

Within a few months, Nana was transferred to a nursing home to finish up her rehab. Nana ended up going to the same facility in Cheektowaga that her sister Jane was at.

I would go several times a week to visit Nana and Aunt Jane.

One day while mom and I were visiting Nana, Nana told us a story about Aunt Jane. "Susan, do you know where Janie went yesterday?"

"No mom, what did Auntie do?"

"Janie told me that she went to Atlantic City last night. She said she took the bus from here and that it was filled with a whole bunch of young hansom men. And she won big on the slots!"

Mom said, "I don't think that happened mom."

"Well why would Janie lie to me Susan? She said she has the money back in her room and that she would show me," Nana replied.

Mom said, "Mom, you've been to Atlantic City before. You know how long it takes to get there. Do you really think she went?"

"I asked Janie why she didn't bring me with her to Atlantic City, and she told me that she forgot to get me."

Mom told Nana again, "Mom, Aunt Jane has dementia, Alzheimer's. She didn't go anywhere last night. She stayed right here."

Nana didn't want to hear anything of the sort.

Aunt Jane ended up passing away in 2008, a few weeks before my wedding.

A few months later, Nana completed her rehab stint at the retirement home.

☺

In 2006, Uncle Michael decided to live out one of his dreams and open up a bar and restaurant. He needed a name for his new establishment, and it seemed like there was only one logical choice; Ziggy's Restaurant and Sports Bar in Wake Forrest, NC.

Every time Grandpa went down to visit Uncle Michael, he was treated like a celebrity at the restaurant. All the patrons and regulars wanted to meet him and shake his hand. Grandpa had no problem telling anyone who would listen to his life story!

☺

In early 2009 Grandpa Ziggy told me, *"Don't call me on the phone no more. I can't really hear too well, you know. Instead, used the email! That's a lot easier for me. I like to read and write…"*

Grandpa Ziggy checked his email multiple times a day. I enjoyed writing to him and receiving his emails. We would write about everything from the Sabres to work to cars to politics to fishing!

Chapter 8
The Ever-Growing Family

On March 6, 2005, Nana and Grandpa Ziggy became great grandparents. My older sister, Sarah, and her husband, Eric, had given birth to their daughter, Hannah. Nana and Grandpa we thrilled to become great grandparents! At one point, Nana told Mom, "Well, Susan, you may be a grandmother, but you don't know what it's like to be a great grandma!" The two of them laughed.

Almost two years later, on December 24, 2006, my older sister Sarah gave birth to a baby boy, Jonah. Nana and Grandpa were thrilled again to be great grandparents! Nana and Grandpa Ziggy enjoyed watching their family grow.

☹

Nana and Grandpa Ziggy have always had a cat. They had Nicholas, who was a mean Siamese. After he died, he was replaced by Sasha, another Siamese, who was not as mean as Nicholas. After Sasha, they had Bruce. Bruce was born on their patio by a stray black cat. I named Bruce after Bruce Smith of the Buffalo Bills because he was the largest kitten of the litter.

One evening, Bruce was ready for bed. Normally he would meow to either Nana or Grandpa Ziggy to let them know he wanted to go in the basement—that's where he was kept during the night; otherwise he would run amuck upstairs. One of them would get up and open the basement door.

Nana got up off the couch and walked down the hall, with Bruce leading the charge.

From the kitchen, there were two stairs down to a landing. The landing had a door for the outside and a door for the basement. Nana leaned from the kitchen to open the basement door for

Bruce. She ended up losing her balance and fell. She called for Grandpa Ziggy and he rushed over to find her lying on the ground. Inevitably, Nana broke her hip.

She ended up having hip replacement surgery at ECMC. The surgery went well. She began rehab again shortly after surgery.

At first, Nana did well with rehab, considering that she was eighty seven. However, as time passed, so did Nana's mental and physical health. She never regained the strength to become well enough to live at home. Additionally, Grandpa—who was eighty two—could not properly care for her at home. Nana would spend the last years of her life at ECMC. Mom and Grandpa Ziggy went practically every day to visit Nana.

As the years went by, so did Nana's memory. One afternoon, I visited Nana along with Mom, Grandpa Ziggy, and my girlfriend Shannon. Grandpa sat in a chair in the corner, reading the paper. We had the TV on for background noise. Nana asked Mom, "Susan. Where is my husband?"

Mom questioned, "Your husband? You mean Dad?"

Nana said, "No, my husband."

Mom pointed at Grandpa. "He's sitting right there, reading the paper."

Nana looked over at Grandpa and blurted out, "That?! I married that? No, Susan! Where's my real husband?"

"Well how many husbands do you have Mom? I only know of the one sitting right here," Mom said.

As amusing as the conversation was, it was sad seeing Nana's memory fade.

☺

On September 13, 2008, Shannon and I got married in downtown Rochester. Sitting in the first pew at church was Nana and Grandpa Ziggy. They were both proud of Shannon and me. At the reception, I was able to break away from Shannon and sneak in a short dance with Nana.

☺

During the summer of 2009 our family had a surprise ninetieth birthday party for Nana. Mom and Uncle Michael wanted to celebrate Nana's life while she was still with us.

The party was held in the basement of the school at St. Josaphat's. Mom busted Nana out of the long-term care ward at ECMC.

All of the family and many friends were at the party, including Nana's friends from Parish Seniors, Holy Name Society, Rosary Society, Justinettes, and ceramics. It was a very good party.

☹

A few months later, Nana's health took a turn for the worse. While still at ECMC, she suffered a stroke during the early hours of the morning.

Mom called me around 9am to tell me the bad news. I left work that moment and drove from Rochester to Buffalo.

When I got to her room, Mom and Grandpa Ziggy were there. Nana was slightly responsive, but she was not awake or talking and her eyes were closed. I held her hand and told her that I was there and that I loved her. Nana squeezed my hand.

There was nothing the hospital staff could do except make her comfortable.

Nana passed away a couple days later on Monday November 6, 2009. The wake and funeral were later that week.

On the morning at the funeral—November 9th—the family gathered at the funeral home for one last viewing. Before the undertaker closed the coffin, I gave Nana seven Lucky 7s scratch-off tickets, one ticket for each grandkid and great grandkid. The Lucky 7s were her favorite scratch-off tickets.

Everyone met at St. Josaphat's for the funeral. After Mass, the family caravanned over to the cemetery, where Nana was laid to rest. There was bereavement breakfast in the same hall that we celebrated Nana's 90th birthday just months earlier.

A few days later, I was at a gas station and I decided to buy a scratch off ticket. I wasn't sure if it was luck or divine intervention, but I won seven dollars on a Lucky 7s ticket.

☺

A few weeks later, the holiday season hit, which was a little rough because it was the first Thanksgiving and Christmas without Nana.

After Christmas, Grandpa asked Uncle Michael if he could spend the winter with him in North Carolina. Grandpa said that each year, the Buffalo winters were harder and harder on his body. Uncle Michael had no issue bringing his father back home with him.

The following spring, Grandpa came back up to his home in Buffalo.

For the next few years, Grandpa would spend the summers living by himself at his home in Cheektowaga and spend the winters down in Carolina.

During 2013, Grandpa got the urge to sell his home. Even though he was eighty-eight, he was still sharp as a tack. Grandpa said, *"I'm only living in this house for a couple months out of the year. And even when I am in Buffalo, I stay at your mother's house so she can watch and take care of me. Why should I pay taxes and utilities on a house that I am not living in? I live with Michael and Susan; there is no reason for me to have my own house anymore."*

I would occasionally help Mom and Uncle Michael help clean out Nana and Grandpa's house, which took a while. There was over fifty years' worth of stuff collecting in that house. The house finally went on the market during the summer of 2014 and it was a sad moment. I had a lot of memories growing up in that house. The house finally sold sometime during 2015.

☺

After Grandpa moved in with Uncle Michael in Raleigh, I had gone down a few times so we could watch our Sabres take on the

Carolina Hurricanes. However, on December 23, 2014, I decided to take Grandpa Ziggy on a small road trip.

At the time, Grandpa was back home in Buffalo. He was staying with Mom for the Thanksgiving and Christmas holidays. He was scheduled to go back to Carolina on New Year's Day.

I had a little boys' trip planned. I was going to take Grandpa Ziggy to Detroit so we could watch our Sabres take on the Red Wings at Joe Louis Arena.

Grandpa and I left Buffalo early in the morning. I had a hot cup of Tim Hortons coffee ready for him. We had a quick drive through Canada. During our ride, I had Grandpa tell me his whole life story again. Even though I had heard the story umpteen million times, there were always some of the smallest details that I forgot. And since I was writing a story about him and Nana, I constantly needed to be refreshed on their narrative of their life.

The mini vacation was memorable, an experience that I will never forget.

I took Grandpa Ziggy to the Henry Ford Museum. He really enjoyed it. He got a little upset when he saw the Lincoln limousine that President Kennedy was assassinated in. However, he lit up when he saw the 1949 Ford 2 door on display! *"Hey Adam! I used to own one of these! This was my first car! This one is green, but I had a maroon one. I was only in this country of ours for three weeks before I had my very own new car…"* Grandpa went on and on about his first Ford, but I did not mind. I enjoy listening to his story, no matter how many times I have heard it. Sadly, I know that there will come a day where hearing the life stories from the horse's mouth will end, but until that time, I will enjoy every minute of it!

For a late lunch/early dinner, I found a nice small Polish diner, Jim's Place, in Dearborn; it was right around the corner from the museum. It was your typical Polish place, right down to the Pope John Paul II picture up on the wall. Grandpa and I feasted on Polish delicacies like Polish sausage, pierogies, stuffed cabbage, and potato pancakes.

We stayed at Greektown Casino and took the people mover over to the Joe.

That season, the Sabres were in full on "Tank Mode." They were horrible and us Sabre fans had "Embraced the Tank!" The Sabres were losing on purpose to try to get a great draft pick.

Anyway, Grandpa Ziggy and I watched the Sabres—who were a bunch of no-names and Rochester Americans—give the Red Wings a run for their money. At one point, the Sabres were winning 3-1, but ended up losing 3-6.

After the game, Grandpa and I took the people mover back to the casino. I grabbed us both a round of Coronas and we played the one-arm bandits for a bit. We decided to call midnight bedtime.

That night, I had a very weird dream...I dreamt that Grandpa Ziggy saw an ultrasound picture of his latest great grandchild and spoiled the surprise on what the sex was. Shannon and I wanted to be surprised on what our baby was going to be, so we did not find out its gender. According to my dream, Grandpa blew the surprise and said it was going to be a boy.

The following morning—Christmas Eve—I woke up being very upset with Grandpa. I could not believe that he would blow such a surprise like that! I was angry for about ten minutes until I realized that it was all a dream. And the only one that knew what the baby was going to be was the Big Man Upstairs!

Later that morning, Grandpa and I gathered our belongings and made our back home to Buffalo. During the trip back, Grandpa told me more of his life story, pausing often to say, *"I've done a lot in my life. I have a lot of stories. I should write a book about my life."*

I would ask Grandpa, "Well, why don't you."

Grandpa would just shrug his shoulders and say, *"Well, I don't know. I don't have the time. Plus, I don't want people to think that I am a traitor or deserter during the War."*

To that, I told him, "I don't think you are a traitor. You were forced to join the German Navy; you didn't have a choice. You had to look out for yourself, it was survival. You didn't even want to fight in the first place. I think you did the right thing and did what you needed to do to survive."

Grandpa said, *"Well I know that. I just don't know if other people will see it that way."*

"Well Grandpa, if they can't see it that way, then they are just plain dumb!"

I got Grandpa back home by early afternoon. I spent some time with Mom before heading back to Rochester. The following day, Mom and Grandpa came over to celebrate Christmas with pregnant Shannon and me. A few days later, Grandpa flew back down to Carolina for the winter.

All throughout Shannon's pregnancy, Grandpa kept telling me, *"Don't let wifey carry anything heavy. Estelle was pregnant one time and she carried something heavy and she ended up having a miscarriage. I don't want the two of yous to lose the baby!"*

On Tuesday, January 13, 2015 Shannon and I welcomed our first child into this world. Parker Zigmund DeRose was born at 5am. Throughout the entire pregnancy, we did not know the sex of the baby, we wanted to be surprised. After thinking about it, I thought it was a bit weird that my dream about having a baby boy came true.

Later that morning, I called Grandpa Ziggy to tell him that he was finally going to have a namesake. Even though Grandpa Ziggy was living with Michael down in Raleigh, Grandpa Ziggy was still very excited! Right off the bat, Grandpa Ziggy started calling his great grandson *"Little Ziggy."*

Grandpa finally got to meet his newest great grandchild and namesake of Friday March 20, 2015. The next day, Shannon and I were having our baby baptized. Since Uncle Michael was my Godfather, I decided to ask him to be my son's Godfather, too. Shannon asked her cousin Jessica to be Little Ziggy's Godmother.

Every month, I would take pictures of Little Ziggy and mail them to Grandpa Ziggy down there in Carolina. Grandpa would mail the pictures of his namesake to the extended family back in Poland. Grandpa still hand wrote letters and emails to his sister, Zosia, and other members of his and Nana's side of the family.

☺

On July 9, 2015 Grandpa Ziggy turned ninety years old. I asked Grandpa what he thought about being ninety and he said, *"It's a nice age, but I would like to see one hundred."*

I asked him if he ever thought he would make it to ninety, considering everything that he went through in life.

Grandpa said, *"I never thought it would come this fast! How old are you? Thirty-one? I would like to be thirty-one again."*

I asked him, "If you were thirty-one again, what would you do?"

"Well," Ziggy said, *"I would probably do some more fishing!"* Fishing was definitely one of his passions.

☺

On Christmas Day 2015, Shannon and I told Grandpa Ziggy that he was going to be a great grandfather again. Yet again, Grandpa was trilled and over joyed. He said, *"I hope you have a girl this time. You already have a boy, so it would be nice to have something different."*

I told him, "Well Grandpa, you just have to wait until August 2016 to find out what we are having!"

☺

On July 9, 2016 Mom, Little Ziggy, and I celebrated Grandpa Ziggy's ninety-first birthday! We went out to lunch at Ruby Tuesday along with his old neighbors Kathy and Jim. It's a little difficult to go birthday present shopping for a ninety-one-year-old. I printed of a bunch of pictures of Little Ziggy for Grandpa so that he could send them to Poland. The other thing I got Grandpa was a rough draft copy of this book!

I spent almost the entire month of June 2016 working on this story for Grandpa. I wanted to have a rough draft in book formation in time for him to open up on his birthday. Grandpa was beyond thrilled to see his story in print.

That day after lunch, Mom and Grandpa ran some errands and then went to church. Mom said as soon as they got home from

Mass, Grandpa sat down on the couch and started to read the book about his life. Naturally, he started with the pictures first!

By Sunday night, Grandpa Ziggy had emailed me, informing me that he really enjoyed the book and greatly appreciated it. His only complaint was for me to add a couple more stories (which I did). Additionally, Grandpa wanted the book translated to Polish so that his relatives back in Old Country could read his story. Lastly, he wanted the profits from the book to go into Little Ziggy's and Baby #2's college funds.

Grandpa Ziggy had always looked out for his children, grandchildren, and great grandchildren's' futures. As soon as my cousins, Alex and Nathan, and my sisters and I were born, Grandpa Ziggy started investing in the stock market for our future. The money earned was to help pay for college. The same went when Little Ziggy was born and he talked about investments for Baby #2.

God always watched over Grandpa Ziggy and Grandpa Ziggy is watching over his family.

☺

At 7pm on Wednesday, July 27, 2016 Shannon and I welcomed Annabelle Catherine into the world. I called Grandpa while Shannon, Annabelle, and I were in the recovery room. Grandpa Ziggy was happy, thrilled, ecstatic, and through the roof! *"Oh, hey! How about that! I was right! I wanted a baby girl! I knew it was going to be a girl! I want to buy her a nice dress. All beautiful girls need a nice dress!"* The following day, Grandpa Ziggy got to meet his fourth great grandchild. Grandpa had a huge smile on his face the moment he laid eyes on Annabelle.

☺

Grandpa Ziggy spends most of his time now living with his son, Michael, and daughter-in-law, Kathy, in Raleigh, North Carolina. At least once a month, Uncle Michael takes Grandpa Ziggy to Myrtle Beach, South Carolina, for quick getaways.

The two of them like to hit up the local happy hour spots. And if you are at the right place at the right time, you just might be sitting in a bar stool next to Grandpa Ziggy! Try to order a cold Molson—because that's his favorite beer—and get ready for him to tell you about his life in Poland, the War, and how much he loves his home of Buffalo, New York.

☺

www.ingramcontent.com/pod-product-compliance
Lightning Source LLC
Chambersburg PA
CBHW071102040426
42443CB00013B/3376